Introduction

I am so excited to bring you this Quilted Skinnies book! These charming Skinnies are quick to make and so versatile. Their small size, 14" x 28", allows them to be used practically anywhere, making them useful for various occasions and holidays. Add to that how fun, bright and upbeat they are, and you have a great creative project.

Skinnies are perfect for the beginner quilter as well as fun and fast for experienced quilters. Using fusible web for the whimsical images takes a lot of the stress out of the sewing and piecing process.

I hope you enjoy making them for yourself and your friends as much as I have enjoyed creating them for you. One more thing—Quilted Skinnies are very addicting, and you will find you can't make just one. So enjoy all these adorable patterns.

Margie

Table of Contents

Haunted Halloween,
page 21

North Pole,
page 27

Meet the Designer

Margie Ullery's mom taught her how to sew when she was a young girl. By the age of 12 she was making her own clothes for school. She made her first quilt at age 14 and still has it today.

In 2008, her love for designing grew and expanded to include quilts. In 2010, Margie started Ribbon Candy Quilt Company. The quilts she designs are for the busy, so her patterns are usually fast and easy. She loves using fusible web appliqué because it's versatile and allows her to create unique images. Margie is well-known for her Seasonal Skinnies patterns, the flagship of Ribbon Candy Quilt Company.

Margie's designs have been in a number of publications, including *Quiltmaker's 100 Blocks*, *Quiltmaker* magazine, *American Patchwork and Quilting 2013* calendar, and the book *Springtime in the Rockies*, with more publications on the way.

Margie was born and raised in central California, but has lived in Utah for the past 18 years. She is married, and a mom to five children. When she isn't sewing, you can find her enjoying time with her family or indulging in other hobbies, which include reading, baking, scrapbooking and making jewelry.

To see more of Margie's designs, visit Ribbon Candy patterns blog at: www.ribboncandyquilts. blogspot.com and "like" her Facebook page at: www.facebook.com/ ribboncandyquiltcompany.

Birdhouse, **page 13**

Hens & Chick, **page 16**

General Instructions

Common techniques and general instructions used to construct the projects in this book are referred to in the patterns and explained here. Take a moment to become acquainted with these before beginning your projects.

Basic Tools & Supplies

- Sewing machine in good working order
- Good-quality all-purpose thread to match fabrics
- Sharp scissors
- Seam ripper
- Straight pins and hand-sewing needles
- Measuring tools
- Air- or water-soluble marking pen
- Steam iron, ironing board and pressing cloth
- Pattern tracing paper
- Rotary cutter, mat and straightedges
- Serger

All cuts are precise. All seams are ¼" unless otherwise stated. All appliqué images are full size and ready to trace onto fusible web.

Embroidery: Embroidered details are used on some projects. Use 3 strands of embroidery floss and knot one end. Use a backstitch on pattern details and letters as indicated on some projects.

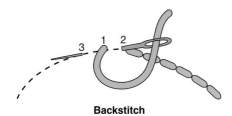

Backstitch

Double-stick fusible web: All projects in this book have been constructed with a double-stick fusible web. This product has a pressure-sensitive adhesive on both sides that allows for a temporary hold; there is no pressing until your entire appliqué design is in place to allow for positioning changes until you are satisfied with the design.

Medium-weight fusible interfacing: When a very light fabric is fused to a darker or printed fabric, the colors from the underneath layers will probably show through the lighter top layer. To avoid this, you may use a medium-weight fusible interfacing on the wrong side of the lighter appliqué fabric before adding the fusible web and cutting shapes.

This extra layer is placed between the background and the appliquéd piece in the finished project.

Fusible Appliqué

Follow these general instructions to prepare templates for appliqué motifs. Refer to the manufacturer's instructions for specifics of fusible web application.

1. If you prewash fabrics, do not use dryer sheets with fabrics that will be fused.

2. Trace appliqué shapes given on the pattern inserts (shapes are given in reverse for this type of appliqué) on the paper liner. Be sure to leave space in between the images so you can cut them out.

3. Cut out each image ¼" from drawn line.

4. Peel off back paper liner and place the sticky side of the fusible web on the wrong side of the fabric. *Note: You will still have the top paper liner that has the drawn image. If a light fabric is being used on top of a dark fabric, apply medium-weight fusible interfacing to the wrong side of these fabrics referring to manufacturer's instructions before applying fusible web.*

5. Using a warm iron, lightly press the fusible web onto the wrong side of the fabric just enough to hold.

6. Let the fabric cool. Transfer all pattern details to fabric using a water-erasable marker.

7. Cut out the images on the drawn line.

8. Trace the complete appliqué motif on a piece of paper with a heavy-line marker. Turn the paper over and trace over the lines to make a right-side–up pattern.

9. Peel off the remaining paper liner and arrange the fabric/fusible web shapes in numerical order, fusible side down on a flat surface, using the traced pattern beneath as a guide for positioning. Move pieces as necessary. *Note: The double-stick fusible web allows you to pick up and move pieces around without fusing.*

10. When satisfied with the placement, center the motif image on the background fabric straight and in proper position.

11. Press the image to the background.

12. Hand- or machine-stitch around all raw edges to secure using a zigzag, satin or blanket stitch or other appliqué or quilting stitch. *Note: Without some kind of edge finish or quilting on top of the pieces, the fused shapes may eventually come off.*

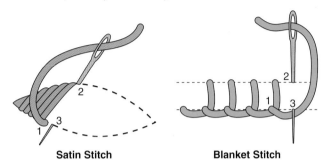

Satin Stitch   **Blanket Stitch**

13. Machine-wash and -dry at low heat.

Quilting

Quilting is the process of sewing two layers of fabric together with a layer of batting between. It adds loft while securing the layers.

1. Sandwich the batting piece between the completed top and the prepared backing piece; press out any wrinkles, and pin or baste the layers together.

2. You may quilt in any design you prefer. You may add as much quilting as is desired, or as recommended by the batting manufacturer.

3. When quilting is complete, trim excess backing and batting even with the edges of the project top to prepare the quilt for binding.

Binding

The projects that require binding as an edge finish in this book use straight-grain binding strips. To prepare and apply binding, refer to the following instructions.

1. Cut binding strips as directed in individual projects.

2. Join the strips on the short ends with diagonal seams to make one long strip; trim seams to ¼" and press open (Figure 1). Cut the starting end on the diagonal and press under ¼".

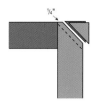

Figure 1

3. Fold the strip along the length with wrong sides together and press to make a double-layered strip (Figure 2).

Figure 2

4. Pin the diagonal end of the binding strip to the back-side raw edge of the project at the center of one side, matching raw edges. Begin to stitch binding to project a short distance from a corner of the project using a ¼" seam, and leaving the diagonal end of binding unstitched. Stop stitching ¼" from corner and backstitch (Figure 3).

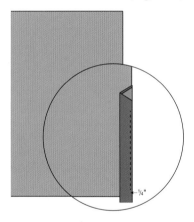

Figure 3

5. Remove quilt from machine and turn. Fold binding up at a 45-degree angle to seam, and then down even with quilt edges forming a pleat at the corner (Figure 4).

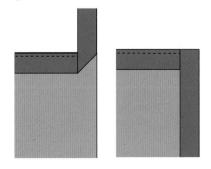

Figure 4

6. Resume stitching at corner, backstitching ¼" from corner (Figure 5). Repeat to starting point.

 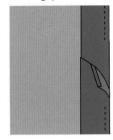

Figure 5   **Figure 6**

7. Cut binding off long enough to tuck inside starting end and complete stitching (Figure 6).

8. Turn binding to quilt front to enclose the seam and stitch in place using a narrow zigzag stitch (Figure 7), mitering each corner (Figure 8).

Figure 7   **Figure 8**

Strip-Piecing Appliqué Pieces

Some Skinny appliqué pieces are strip-pieced to add charm and variation to the quilt. The strips are cut in a variety of widths so you can use smaller fabric pieces from your stash. The widths of the strips range from 1–2½" with the length varying depending on the size of the appliqué piece.

Follow these instructions to prepare strip-pieced motifs.

1. Measure the length or width of the appliqué piece you want to strip piece. Add 1" to this measurement and cut each strip to this length.

2. Sew two strips, right sides together. Continue adding strips, varying the strip widths until the pieced rectangle is large enough to cover the appliqué piece referring to Figure 9. Press all seams to one side.

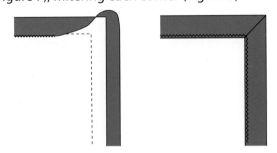

Figure 9

3. Prepare appliqué piece in same manner as with single fabric.

Finishing Your Skinny
Each of the Skinnies in this book is finished in the same manner. Refer to the following instructions.

Cutting

From border fabric:
• Cut 2 (2½" by fabric width) strips
  Subcut each strip into one 2½" x 24½" A strip and one 2½" x 14½" B strip.

From binding fabric:
• Cut 3 (2¼" by fabric width) strips

Completing the Quilt
1. Sew the A strips to opposite long sides of the quilt center referring to Figure 10. Press seams toward the A strips.

2. Sew the B strips to the top and bottom of the pieced center to complete the quilt top again referring to Figure 10. Press seams toward the B strips.

3. Press quilt top on both sides; check for proper seam pressing and trim all loose threads.

Figure 10

4. Sandwich batting between the stitched top and the prepared backing piece; pin or baste layers together to hold. Mark quilting design and quilt as desired by hand or machine.

5. When quilting is complete, remove pins or basting. Trim batting and backing fabric edges even with raw edges of quilt top.

6. Join binding strips on short ends with diagonal seams to make one long strip; trim seams to ¼" and press seams open.

7. Fold the binding strip in half with wrong sides together along length; press.

8. Sew binding to quilt edges, matching raw edges, mitering corners and overlapping ends.

9. Fold binding to the back side and stitch in place to finish. ■

Quilted Skinnies for All Seasons

Ollie Owl

Ollie's large eyes and innocent expression will bring smiles to everyone's faces.

Specifications
Skill Level: Confident Beginner
Quilt: 14" x 28"

Materials
- Cotton scraps:
    Yellow and brown prints
    White solid
    4 different light coral tonals or prints
- ¼ yard dark coral tonal
- ¼ yard light coral print (binding)
- ⅓ yard coordinating flower print (borders)
- ½ yard white tonal
- Backing to size
- Batting to size
- Thread
- ⅝ yard 18"-wide double-stick fusible web
- Basic sewing tools and supplies

Cutting
Refer to General Instructions on page 3 for preparing and using patterns given on the pattern insert. Transfer all pattern markings to fabric. Use appliqué motif and pieces for Ollie Owl.

From yellow print:
- Cut appliqué motif pieces for beak and feet.

From brown print:
- Cut appliqué motif piece for pupils and branch.

From white solid:
- Cut appliqué motif pieces for inner eyes.

From light coral tonals or prints:
- Cut appliqué motif pieces for outer eyes and 10 chest feathers.

From dark coral tonal:
- Cut appliqué motif pieces for head, body, wings and tail.

From white tonal:
- Cut 1 (10½" x 24½") background rectangle.

Completing the Skinny
Refer to General Instructions on page 3 for Fusible Appliqué techniques.

1. Prepare the appliqué motif pieces for Ollie Owl, tail and branch.

2. Center the 10 chest feathers on the background rectangle, starting approximately 8½" from bottom and layering them on top of each other, referring to Figure 1. Fuse center of each strip to hold in place.

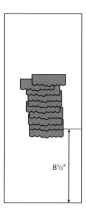

8½"

Figure 1

3. Add owl body, wings and head referring to Figure 2; trimming ends of chest feather strips as needed. Continue to add the owl motif pieces in numerical order, except for feet.

Figure 2

4. Position the branch over the body and tail referring to the placement diagram, trimming branch ends even with background rectangle.

5. Add the feet motif pieces over the branch referring to placement diagram for positioning.

6. When satisfied with placement, fuse pieces in place.

7. Stitch pieces in place beginning with the lowest piece in a layered section using a machine blanket stitch and matching thread.

8. Add borders, quilt and bind referring to Finishing Your Skinny on page 5. ■

Ollie Owl
Placement Diagram 14" x 28"

Easter Chick

"Are my ears too big?" This cute chick is doing his best to imitate the Easter Bunny with his pile of eggs and big bunny ears.

Specifications
Skill Level: Confident Beginner
Quilt: 14" x 28"

Materials
- Cotton scraps:
    White, pink and yellow tonals
    Yellow polka dot
    Orange solid
    Green print
    Pink, blue, orange, yellow and purple prints
        and green tonal (eggs)
- ¼ yard coordinating stripe (binding)
- ⅓ yard pink print (borders)
- ½ yard pink on white print
- Backing to size
- Batting to size
- Thread
- 2 (³⁄₁₆") black buttons
- ⅝ yard 18"-wide double-stick fusible web
- Basic sewing tools and supplies

Cutting
Refer to General Instructions on page 3 for preparing and using patterns given on the pattern insert. Transfer all pattern markings to fabric. Use appliqué pieces or motifs for Easter Chick.

From white tonal:
- Cut appliqué motif piece for bunny ears.

From pink tonal:
- Cut appliqué motif pieces for inner ears 1 and 2.

From yellow tonal:
- Cut appliqué motif piece for chick body.

From yellow polka dot:
- Cut appliqué motif pieces for chick wings.

From orange solid:
- Cut appliqué motif pieces for chick feet and beak.

From green print:
- Cut appliqué motif pieces for grass 1 and 2.

From prints (for eggs):
- Cut appliqué motif pieces for 6 eggs. *Note: 2 of the eggs in the sample quilt were strip-pieced. Refer to Strip-Piecing Appliqué Pieces on page 5 in General Instructions to prepare, or use single fabric piece.*

From pink on white print:
- Cut 1 (10½" x 24½") background rectangle.

Completing the Skinny
Refer to General Instructions on page 3 for Fusible Appliqué techniques.

1. Prepare the appliqué motif pieces for the chick, six eggs, grass 1 and grass 2.

2. Arrange the six eggs on the background rectangle, referring to the Placement Diagram and the photo.

3. Arrange grass 1 and grass 2 pieces on top of the bottom eggs referring to the placement diagram. Add the chick motif on top of the stacked eggs referring to Placement Diagram for positioning.

4. When satisfied with placement, fuse pieces in place.

5. Stitch pieces in place beginning with the lowest piece in a layered section using a machine blanket stitch and matching thread.

6. Add borders, quilt and bind referring to Finishing Your Skinny on page 5 in General Instructions.

7. Sew buttons on chick where marked for eyes. ∎

Easter Chick
Placement Diagram 14" x 28"

Beach Chair

Picture yourself relaxed in this comfortable beach chair by the water.

Specifications
Skill Level: Confident Beginner
Quilt: 14" x 28"

Materials
- Cotton scraps:
    White and light blue tonals
    Yellow, orange, green and red tonals
    Medium and dark blue tonals
    Tan tonal and tan batik
    Yellow print
- ¼ yard dark blue dot (binding)
- ⅓ yard orange batik (borders)
- ½ yard orange dot
- Backing to size
- Batting to size
- Thread
- ⅝ yard 18"-wide double-stick fusible web
- Basic sewing tools and supplies

Cutting
Refer to General Instructions on page 3 for preparing and using patterns given on the pattern insert. Transfer all pattern markings to fabric. Use appliqué motifs and pieces for chair, sand/ocean, umbrella, umbrella pole and top, sun, and large and small sun rays.

From white tonal:
- Cut appliqué motif piece for surf foam.

From light blue tonal:
- Cut appliqué motif piece for ocean.

From yellow, orange, green and red tonals:
- Cut appliqué motif pieces from each color for umbrella 1, 2, 3 and 5 sections. Cut appliqué motif piece from green for umbrella pole and top.

From medium blue tonal:
- Cut appliqué motif pieces for chair handles 1 and 2 and back and front legs 1 and 2.

From dark blue tonal:
- Cut appliqué motif pieces for chair back/seat and umbrella 4 section.

From tan tonal:
- Cut appliqué motif piece for sand 2.

From tan batik:
- Cut appliqué motif pieces for sands 1 and 3.

From yellow print:
- Cut appliqué motif pieces for sun, 6 small rays and 6 large rays.

From orange dot:
- Cut 1 (10½" x 24½") background rectangle.

Completing the Skinny
Refer to General Instructions on page 3 for Fusible Appliqué techniques.

1. Prepare the appliqué motif pieces for the chair, sand/ocean, umbrella, umbrella pole and top, sun, and small and large sun rays.

2. Arrange the sand/ocean motif at the bottom of the background rectangle referring to Figure 1. Trim ends even with background fabric.

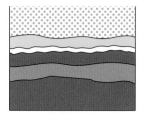

Figure 1

3. Fuse pieces in place and then stitch pieces in place using a machine blanket stitch and matching thread.

4. Arrange the five umbrella pieces on the background and then tuck the top pole piece under the umbrella pieces and the pole under the bottom of the orange umbrella section referring to the placement diagram for positioning.

5. Add the chair, sun and sun ray pieces referring to placement diagram for positioning.

6. When satisfied with placement, fuse pieces in place.

7. Stitch pieces in place beginning with the lowest piece in a layered section using a machine blanket stitch and matching thread.

8. Add borders, quilt and bind referring to Finishing Your Skinny on page 5. ■

Beach Chair
Placement Diagram 14" x 28"

Birdhouse

Welcome spring with this cute birdhouse and flowerpot. The flowering vine adds additional color and is sure to chase away those winter blues.

Specifications
Skill Level: Confident Beginner
Quilt: 14" x 28"

Materials
- Cotton scraps:
  Blue print
  Yellow print
  Green and purple tonals
  Pink and brown prints
  Blue tonals
  Yellow tonals
- ¼ yard green plaid (binding)
- ⅓ yard flower print (borders)
- ½ yard white tonal
- Backing to size
- Batting to size
- Thread
- 6 (⅝") yellow buttons
- ⅝ yard 18"-wide double-stick fusible web
- Basic sewing tools and supplies

Cutting
Refer to General Instructions on page 3 for preparing and using patterns given on the pattern insert. Transfer all pattern markings to fabric. Use appliqué motifs or pieces for birdhouse.

From blue print:
- Cut appliqué motif piece for roof.

From yellow print:
- Cut appliqué motif piece for pot lip.

From green tonal:
- Cut appliqué motif pieces for 11 leaves, 2 grasses and 1 vine.

From purple tonal:
- Cut appliqué motif pieces for 3 flowers.

From pink print:
- Cut appliqué motif pieces for 3 flowers.

From brown print:
- Cut appliqué motif piece for post.

From blue tonals:
- Cut appliqué motif piece for house. *Note: The house is strip-pieced using several blue tonal fabrics. Refer to Strip-Piecing Appliqué Pieces on page 5 to prepare.*

From yellow tonals:
- Cut appliqué motif piece for house door and pot body. *Note: The pot body is strip-pieced using several yellow tonal fabrics. Refer to Strip-Piecing Appliqué Pieces on page 5 to prepare.*

From white tonal:
- Cut 1 (10½" x 24½") background rectangle.

Completing the Skinny

Refer to General Instructions on page 3 for Fusible Appliqué techniques.

1. Prepare the appliqué motif pieces for the house, flowerpot, post, vine, six flowers, 11 leaves and two grasses.

2. Center the house, post and flowerpot on the background rectangle tucking the ends of the post underneath the house and flowerpot, referring to the placement diagram and photo.

3. Add the vine to the post placing the vine behind the post near the top, referring to photo.

4. Add flowers, leaves and grass referring to placement diagram for positioning.

5. When satisfied with placement, fuse pieces in place.

6. Stitch pieces in place beginning with the lowest piece in a layered section using a machine blanket stitch and matching thread.

7. Add borders, quilt and bind referring to Finishing Your Skinny on page 5.

8. Sew one button in the center of each flower. ■

Birdhouse
Placement Diagram 14" x 28"

Hens & Chick

Create this fun Hens & Chick Skinny with a little black-and-white fabric and some splashes of color.

Specifications
Skill Level: Confident Beginner
Quilt: 14" x 28"

Materials
- Cotton scraps:
    Yellow, red and blue prints
    Green tonal
    Black polka dot
    Black print
    Several black-and-white prints
- ¼ yard black print (binding)
- ⅓ yard black-on-white print (borders)
- ½ yard white solid
- Backing to size
- Batting to size
- Thread
- Black embroidery floss
- 2 (⅛") black buttons
- 2 (⁵⁄₁₆") black buttons
- 3 (½") yellow buttons
- 14" green narrow rickrack
- ⅝ yard 18"-wide double-stick fusible web
- Basic sewing tools and supplies

Cutting
Refer to General Instructions on page 3 for preparing and using patterns given on the pattern insert. Transfer all pattern markings to fabric. Use appliqué motifs or pieces for large hen, medium hen, small chick, leaf and flower.

From yellow print:
- Cut appliqué motif pieces for large beak, medium beak and chick beak.

From red print:
- Cut appliqué motif pieces for large comb, medium comb and chick comb.

From blue print:
- Cut appliqué motif pieces for 3 flowers.

From green tonal:
- Cut appliqué motif pieces for 5 leaves.

From black polka dot:
- Cut appliqué motif piece for medium body.

From black print:
- Cut appliqué motif piece for large body.

From black-and-white prints:
- Cut appliqué motif pieces for large head, wings and tail; medium head, wings and tail; and chick body and wings. *Note: Select black-and-white prints that will give you a good contrast between adjoining pieces.*

From white solid:
- Cut 1 (10½" x 24½") background rectangle.

Completing the Skinny
Refer to General Instructions on page 3 for Fusible Appliqué and Embroidery techniques.

1. Prepare the appliqué motif pieces for large hen, medium hen, chick, three flowers and five leaves.

2. Arrange the large and medium hens and the chick on the background rectangle, referring to the placement diagram for positioning.

3. Position the flowers on either side of the chick referring to the photo below. Lightly pencil a line for the stem of each flower, and position the leaves tucking one under the wing of the chick.

18

4. Measure flower stem lengths as drawn and cut rickrack to these lengths. Insert and pin rickrack under the bottom edge of each flower.

5. When satisfied with placement, fuse pieces in place. *Note: Remove pins holding rickrack as you fuse the flowers.*

6. Stitch pieces in place beginning with the lowest piece in a layered section using a machine blanket stitch and matching thread. Sew the rickrack in place over stem lines.

7. With a pencil lightly trace the large and medium hen legs onto the background fabric. Using black embroidery floss backstitch hen legs.

8. Add borders, quilt and bind referring to Finishing Your Skinny on page 5.

9. Sew the two smaller black buttons on chick where marked for eyes. Sew one larger black button each on large and medium hens for eyes. Sew yellow button in the center of each flower. ■

Hens & Chick
Placement Diagram 14" x 28"

Pumpkins for Sale

Welcome autumn with this colorful and fun pumpkin patch Skinny.

Specifications
Skill Level: Confident Beginner
Quilt: 14" x 28"

Materials
- Cotton scraps:
    Light green, dark green, gold, dark orange,
      red and medium brown tonals
    Dark brown, medium green and gold prints
    3 different orange prints or tonals
    Tan tonal
- ¼ yard orange print (binding)
- ⅓ yard coordinating flower print (borders)
- ½ yard cream tonal
- Backing to size
- Batting to size
- Thread
- Dark brown embroidery floss
- ⅝ yard 18"-wide double-stick fusible web
- Basic sewing tools and supplies

Cutting
Refer to General Instructions on page 3 for preparing and using patterns given on the pattern insert. Transfer all pattern markings to fabric. Use appliqué pieces or motifs for branch, sign, post, small leaf, oak leaf, maple leaf, sunflower and stem, tall and fat pumpkins and stems.

From gold tonal:
- Cut appliqué motif pieces for 2 small leaves, 1 maple leaf and 1 oak leaf.

From dark orange tonal:
- Cut appliqué motif pieces for 2 small leaves and 1 oak leaf.

From red tonal:
- Cut appliqué motif piece for 1 maple leaf.

From light green tonal:
- Cut appliqué motif pieces for 3 small leaves.

From dark green tonal:
- Cut appliqué motif pieces for 3 small leaves and flower stem.

From medium brown tonal:
• Cut appliqué motif piece for 1 maple leaf.

From dark brown print:
• Cut appliqué motif pieces for branch and flower center.

From medium green print:
• Cut appliqué motif pieces for 1 oak leaf and 3 pumpkin stems.

From gold print or tonals:
• Cut appliqué motif piece for sunflower.

From orange prints:
• Cut appliqué motif pieces for 2 fat pumpkins and 1 tall pumpkin, 1 from each fabric.

From tan tonal:
• Cut appliqué motif pieces for sign and post.

From cream tonal:
• Cut 1 (10½" x 24½") background rectangle.

Completing the Skinny
Refer to General Instructions on page 3 for Fusible Appliqué techniques.

1. Prepare the appliqué motif pieces for branch, sign and post, sunflower, flower center, flower stem, 10 small leaves, three oak leaves, three maple leaves, three pumpkins and stems.

2. Arrange the three pumpkins and stems along with the oak leaves and maple leaves on the background rectangle in numerical order as shown in Figure 1.

Figure 1

3. Arrange sign and post tucking the post under the bottom of the sign and the tall pumpkin, referring to the placement diagram for positioning.

4. Add the sunflower, flower center and stem and three small leaves in numerical order as shown in Figure 2.

Figure 2

5. Add the branch and seven small leaves referring to placement diagram.

6. When satisfied with placement, fuse pieces in place.

7. Stitch pieces in place beginning with the lowest piece in a layered section using a machine blanket stitch and matching thread.

8. With a pencil lightly trace the words on sign. Using dark brown embroidery floss, backstitch the traced words.

9. Add borders, quilt and bind referring to Finishing Your Skinny on page 5. ■

Pumpkins for Sale
Placement Diagram 14" x 28"

Haunted Halloween

Add a little "spooky" to your home at Halloween.

Specifications
Skill Level: Confident Beginner
Quilt: 14" x 28"

Materials
- Cotton scraps:
    Orange, green, gray, black and dark purple prints
    Lavender polka dot
    Yellow, gold, white, dark gray and black tonals
- ¼ yard coordinating stripe (binding)
- ⅓ yard purple and black dot (borders)
- ½ yard lavender tonal
- Backing to size
- Batting to size
- Thread
- 1 (⅜") black button
- ⅝ yard 18"-wide double-stick fusible web
- Basic sewing tools and supplies

Cutting
Refer to General Instructions on page 3 for preparing and using patterns given on the pattern insert. Transfer all pattern markings to fabric. Use appliqué pieces and motifs for the haunted house, ghost and moon.

From orange print:
- Cut appliqué motif piece for jack-o'-lantern.

From green print:
- Cut appliqué motif piece for jack-o'-lantern stem.

From gray print:
- Cut appliqué motif piece for chimney.

From black print:
- Cut appliqué motif pieces for porch and second floor.

From dark purple print:
- Cut appliqué motif pieces for porch roof and step, house roof, second floor roof and shutters.

From lavender polka dot:
- Cut appliqué motif piece for door.

From yellow tonal:
- Cut appliqué motif pieces for second floor window and house windows 1 and 2.

From gold tonal:
- Cut appliqué motif piece for moon.

From white tonal:
- Cut appliqué motif piece for ghost.

From black tonal:
- Cut appliqué motif pieces for ghost face, jack-o'-lantern face and window frames 1 and 2.

From black and dark gray tonals:
- Cut appliqué motif piece for the house. *Note: The house piece in the sample quilt was strip-pieced. Refer to Strip-Piecing Appliqué Pieces on page 5 to prepare or use single fabric piece.*

From lavender tonal:
- Cut 1 (10½" x 24½") background rectangle.

Completing the Skinny

Refer to General Instructions on page 3 for Fusible Appliqué techniques.

1. Prepare the appliqué motif pieces for the moon, ghost and haunted house.

2. Arrange the haunted house and ghost motifs and moon on the background rectangle referring to placement diagram for positioning.

3. When satisfied with placement, fuse pieces in place.

4. Stitch pieces in place beginning with the lowest piece in a layered section using a machine blanket stitch and matching thread.

5. Add borders, quilt and bind referring to Finishing Your Skinny on page 5.

6. Sew button on door where marked. ■

Haunted Halloween
Placement Diagram 14" x 28"

Under the Cornstalk

Perfect for Thanksgiving, this motif of cornstalk and pumpkins
will make an excellent addition to your holiday decor.

Specifications
Skill Level: Confident Beginner
Quilt: 14" x 28"

Materials
- Cotton scraps:
    Dark brown, tan, gold, orange, dark orange,
      green, medium green, dark green and
      yellow prints
- ¼ yard gold plaid (binding)
- ⅓ yard coordinating flower print (borders)
- ½ yard tan tonal
- Backing to size
- Batting to size
- Thread
- ⅝ yard 18"-wide double-stick fusible web
- Basic sewing tools and supplies

Cutting
Refer to General Instructions on page 3 for
preparing and using patterns given on the pattern
insert. Transfer all pattern markings to fabric. Use
appliqué motifs and pieces for cornstalk, pumpkin,
acorns and maple leaves.

From dark brown print:
- Cut appliqué motif pieces for 2 acorn tops.

From tan print:
- Cut appliqué motif pieces for tassel and
  2 acorn bottoms.

From gold, dark orange and green prints:
- Cut 1 maple leaf appliqué motif piece from
  each color.

From orange print:
- Cut appliqué motif piece for pumpkin.

From dark green print:
- Cut appliqué motif piece for pumpkin stem.

From medium green print:
- Cut appliqué motif pieces for cornstalk, 2 corn
  husk 2, and 1 each corn husks 1 and 3.

24

From yellow print:
• Cut appliqué motif pieces for 4 corn ears.

From tan tonal:
• Cut 1 (10½" x 24½") background rectangle.

Completing the Skinny
Refer to General Instructions on page 3 for Fusible Appliqué techniques.

1. Prepare the appliqué motif pieces for cornstalk, pumpkin, three maple leaves and two acorns.

2. Center cornstalk motif with tassel at top on background rectangle referring to the placement diagram for positioning.

3. Arrange the pumpkin, stem, three maple leaves and two acorns, overlapping in numerical order referring to Figure 1.

Figure 1

4. When satisfied with placement, fuse pieces in place.

5. Stitch pieces in place beginning with the lowest piece in a layered section using a machine blanket stitch and matching thread.

6. Add borders, quilt and bind referring to Finishing Your Skinny on page 5. ■

Under the Cornstalk
Placement Diagram 14" x 28"

North Pole

Create this cheery North Pole scene to give as a gift for the holidays.

Specifications
Skill Level: Confident Beginner
Quilt: 14" x 28"

Materials
- Cotton scraps:
    Dark green, medium green and light
      green tonals
    White tonal
    Red tonal
    Green stripe and dot
    Red print
    Red-and-green stripe
- 2 fat quarters different white tonals
- ¼ yard coordinating stripe (binding)
- ⅓ yard red print (borders)
- ½ yard blue star print
- Backing to size
- Batting to size
- Thread
- Black embroidery floss
- 24" red polka dot ribbon
- 12" green ribbon
- 24" red sheer ribbon
- 4 (1") snowflake buttons
- 6 (⅞") snowflake buttons
- ⅝ yard 18"-wide double-stick fusible web
- Basic sewing tools and supplies

Cutting
Refer to General Instructions on page 3 for preparing and using patterns given on the pattern insert. Transfer all pattern markings to fabric. Use appliqué motifs and pieces for striped pole, trees, snows 1, 2 and 3 and gifts 1, 2 and 3.

From dark green tonal:
- Cut appliqué motif piece for tall tree.

From medium green tonal:
- Cut appliqué motif piece for short tree.

From light green tonal:
- Cut appliqué motif piece for gift 2 ribbon.

From white tonal:
- Cut appliqué motif pieces for pole snow patch, sign snow patch and 2 treetop snow patches.

From red tonal:
- Cut appliqué motif pieces for pole top and 5 pole stripes.

From green stripe:
- Cut appliqué motif pieces for gift 1 top and bottom.

From green dot:
- Cut appliqué motif piece for gift 1 rim.

From red print:
- Cut appliqué motif piece for gift 2 box.

From red-and-green stripe:
- Cut appliqué motif piece for gift 3.

From white tonal fat quarters:
- Cut appliqué motif pieces for snows 1 and 3 from one fat quarter. Cut appliqué motif pieces for snow 2, pole and sign from second fat quarter.

From blue star print:
- Cut 1 (10½" x 24½") background rectangle.

Completing the Skinny
Refer to General Instructions on page 3 for Fusible Appliqué and Embroidery techniques.

1. Prepare the appliqué motif pieces for striped pole, tall and short trees, two treetop snow patches, snows 1, 2 and 3 and gifts 1, 2 and 3. Also cut a 4½" piece of polka dot ribbon and prepare for fusing for gift 3.

2. Arrange the snow 1, snow 2 and snow 3 pieces on the background rectangle in numerical order referring to Figure 1.

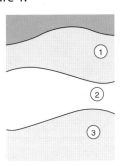

Figure 1

3. Fuse and stitch in place using a machine blanket stitch and matching thread. Trim sides even with background rectangle.

4. Arrange the tall tree and short tree with bottom of tall tree 10" from bottom of background rectangle, referring to Figure 2. The short tree will extend off the background rectangle. Add the treetop snow patches to the top of each tree. Trim right side of short tree even with the background rectangle referring again to Figure 2.

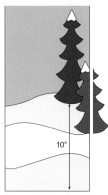

Figure 2

5. Center the striped pole motif referring to placement diagram for positioning.

6. Add gifts 1, 2 and 3 referring to placement diagram for positioning. Add red polka dot ribbon strip to gift 3 as marked.

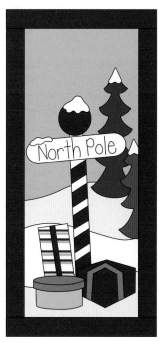

North Pole
Placement Diagram 14" x 28"

7. When satisfied with placement of all motifs, fuse pieces in place.

8. Stitch pieces in place beginning with the lowest piece in a layered section using a machine blanket stitch and matching thread.

9. With a pencil lightly trace the words on the sign. Using black embroidery floss, backstitch the traced words. Using red embroidery floss, backstitch edges of gift 2 box on lines marked in red on appliqué pattern.

10. Add borders, quilt and bind referring to Finishing Your Skinny on page 5.

11. Sew snowflake buttons in sky referring to photo for positioning.

12. Tie a simple bow with the green ribbon and sew in place on gift 1.

13. Tie a bow with several loops using the red sheer ribbon and sew in place on gift 2.

14. Using the red polka dot ribbon make five loops all the same size. Spread them out evenly and tack in place referring photo. Cut a 1½" piece of ribbon and make a circle, sewing the ends together. Sew over the bottom edge of the ribbon loops. Sew ribbon unit to top of gift 3. ■

Smiling Snowflakes

These smiling snowflakes will help you welcome the first snowfall of the season.

Specifications
Skill Level: Confident Beginner
Quilt: 14" x 28"

Materials
- Cotton scraps:
    - 3 different white tonals
    - 3 different orange prints
- ¼ yard dark blue tonal (binding)
- ⅓ yard dark blue tonal (borders)
- ½ yard light blue tonal
- Backing to size
- Batting to size
- Thread
- Black embroidery floss
- 7 (³⁄₁₆") black buttons
- 6 (⁵⁄₁₆") black buttons
- 5 (⅞") snowflake buttons
- 4 (1") snowflake buttons
- ⅝ yard 18"-wide double-stick fusible web
- Basic sewing tools and supplies

Cutting
Refer to General Instructions on page 3 for preparing and using patterns given on the pattern insert. Transfer all pattern markings to fabric. Use patterns for snowflakes 1, 2 and 3.

From white tonals:
- Cut appliqué motif pieces for each of the 3 snowflakes. *Note: Each snowflake in the sample used a different white tonal fabric as well as a different orange print for each nose.*

From orange prints:
- Cut appliqué motif pieces for noses 1, 2 and 3.

From light blue tonal:
- Cut 1 (10½" x 24½") background rectangle.

Completing the Skinny

Refer to General Instructions on page 3 for Fusible Appliqué and Embroidery techniques.

1. Prepare the appliqué motif pieces for snowflakes 1, 2 and 3.

2. Arrange the three snowflakes on the background referring to the placement diagram for positioning.

3. When satisfied with placement, fuse pieces in place.

4. Stitch pieces in place using a machine blanket stitch and matching thread.

5. Using black embroidery floss, backstitch mouths and eyebrows where indicated on motifs.

6. Add borders, quilt and bind referring to Finishing Your Skinny on page 5.

7. Sew two 5/16" black buttons on each snowflake where indicated for eyes. Sew the smaller black buttons on snowflake 1 where indicated for mouth.

8. Sew all the snowflake buttons onto background referring to photo for positioning or as desired. ■

Smiling Snowflakes
Placement Diagram 14" x 28"

Photo Index

Special Thanks

All projects were quilted by Brandy Mascher with the blanket stitching done by Karlene Riggs.

We would like to thank the following manufacturers who provided these materials for this book.

Lite Steam-A-Seam 2 double-stick fusible web from The Warm Company

Warm and Natural Batting from The Warm Company

All buttons from Hill Creek Designs

All thread from Aurifil

Easter Chick,
page 8

Under the Cornstalk,
page 23

Quilted Skinnies for All Seasons is published by Annie's, 306 East Parr Road, Berne, IN 46711. Printed in USA. Copyright © 2014 Annie's. All rights reserved. This publication may not be reproduced in part or in whole without written permission from the publisher.

RETAIL STORES: If you would like to carry this pattern book or any other Annie's publication, visit AnniesWSL.com.

Every effort has been made to ensure that the instructions in this pattern book are complete and accurate. We cannot, however, take responsibility for human error, typographical mistakes or variations in individual work. Please visit AnniesCustomerCare.com to check for pattern updates.

ISBN: 978-1-57367-366-2
3 4 5 6 7 8 9